This book belongs to :

____

____

For my Dad

Published by Miss Daisy Books © 2024

Story © 2024 Tina O Rourke
Illustrations © 2024 Alan Fitzpatrick

The right of Tina O Rourke and Alan Fitzpatrick to be identified as author and illustrator, respectively, of this work has been asserted in accordance with the Copyright, Designs and Patents Act 1988.

All rights reserved. No part of this book may be reproduced, transmitted or stored in an information retrieval system in any form or by any means, graphic, electronic or mechanical, including photocopying, taping and recording without prior written permission from the publisher.

ISBN 978-1-7384679-1-4

www.missdaisybooks.com

A Python
lives
in my Garden

Story by Tina O Rourke
Illustrations by Alan Fitzpatrick

A Python lives in my garden.

It arrived in the middle of the night three weeks ago,
its big Python head looking in my bedroom window.

EXPLORE
EVEREST.

Luckily, I'm not afraid of snakes.
Mum gave me the Giant Encyclopaedia of Snakes for my birthday last year.
Since reading it, I consider myself an authority.

The Python thinks no one knows it's there, but everybody knows.
They know because I tell them. There is only one problem!
No one believes me!

'Billy, have you seen the cat?' Mum asks.

'No, the Python ate her,' I tell Mum.
Just like it ate the Fitzsimons' cat and the Kane's Chihuahua.

'What!
A Python in the garden?
Billy, what an imagination you have.'

But there is a Python.
It keeps swallowing up the neighbours' cats and dogs.

Why doesn't anyone believe me?

Well, enough is enough!
I will capture the Python, and everyone will see.

First, I need to find where it sleeps.
Second, I need a pair of big thick gloves, like the ones Mum wears in the garden.
Third, I need a big bucket and a huge rock.

Capture Python Plan

Mum asks why I need her gloves. I tell her they are for my capture Python plan.

'They're in the garden shed. Just put them back when you are finished,' she smiles.

Dad asks why I need the bucket. I tell him it is for my capture Python plan.

He asks Mum if she knows about the Python in the garden. She tells him, 'Oh yes, Billy has mentioned it.'

'Must be his imaginary friend,' Dad says.
Friend? Who has a Python for a friend?

I ask the next-door neighbour, John, if I can take a rock from his garden.
He nods yes and asks, 'Billy, why do you need a rock?'
I tell him it is for my capture Python plan.

I pick out the most giant rock
I can lift and take it home.

At that moment, I see the Python slithering down the garden.

Its body has a funny shape.
It looks like the O'Brien's Cocker Spaniel is in its tummy.

I hide and watch as it slowly disappears behind the garden shed.

I put on my gloves and sneak over with the bucket and the rock.

I drop the rock
and run towards the Python,
shouting loudly.

The Python twists into a coil, apart from the
dog in its belly.

The Python freezes, and I slam the bucket over its head.
Its tail slithers underneath as the bucket hits the ground.
I did it. I caught the Python. Now, everyone is going to believe me.

I put the rock on the bucket to ensure it can't escape.

'Billy, dinner time, come on in,' Mum calls from the kitchen door.

'Mum, guess what?'

At the same time, Mum's phone pings.
She looks at the message and then at me.

'A Python escaped from a local pet shop and has been spotted in the area.
Billy, is there really a Python in the garden?'

'Yes, I told you, but it's ok now.
The Python is under a bucket with a rock on it.'
Finally, someone believes me.

Mum phoned the pet shop owner and a few hours later they arrived to collect the Python.

They were so happy to get the Python back they awarded me
an honorary snake-handling certificate.

**No Pets (cats or dogs) were actually eaten by the Python
during the telling of this story.**

START 2.
START 1.
START 3.
START 4.
Fido

WORD SEARCH

```
B U C K E T L M Q
T N P Q H O U S E
M F G A R D E N Z
P O C R O C K A B
D Y P A H I F K I
E L T L T R E E L
D A D H M P N N L
S D O R O A C I Y
Y O G P Y N E E L
```

BUCKET   PYTHON   ROCK

GARDEN   TREE   DOG

SNAKE   CAT   HOUSE

FENCE   BILLY   SHED

Visit our website for fun games, colouring sheets and free downloadable resources to complement this story.

www.missdaisybooks.com/apythonlivesinmygarden